SIX

Zaffar Kunial

SIX

FABER & FABER

First published in 2019
by Faber & Faber Ltd
Bloomsbury House
74–77 Great Russell Street
London WC1B 3DA

Typeset by Country Setting, Kingsdown CT14 8ES
Printed in England by CPI Group (UK) Ltd, Croydon CRO 4YY

'Fielder' and 'Six' were first published in *Us* (Faber & Faber, 2018)
'*Made In . . .*' was first published in *The Guardian* (20 April 2019)

A CIP record for this book is available from the British Library

ISBN 978–0–571–35882–3

2 4 6 8 10 9 7 5 3 1

Contents

Mid On . . .

'In the middle, out beyond
right and its opposite' –
(Rumi is said to have said) – 'there is a field' . . .

The Persian for field is Maidan.
I'd like to add my words on that field.
Same time, same place . . . 'I'll meet you on it.'

The Opener

was out early and I came in
for my first innings
at number three, Gower's
number, and my batting had shadows
of his lazy grace, studied
on the square telly, and echoed
in our framed oval mirror
only I was right-handed, so I
was proud in two directions – at going
in, and at being
out, off the thinnest of edges
like Gower
a butterfly whisper
after a couple of elegant air shots
wafting my bat
playing a perhapser
away from the body
out in limbo, in the corridor
of uncertainty, then darting a look behind –
the ball thrown like confetti to the heavens
half in celebration, half in
appeal, which is where I
pause the action –
head turning, west to east
ears half hearing the word *Out*
slowed down, mid-stop, like a deer's
voice sounds, mouth open, caught –
a gaping field, some foreign
corner of my eye clocking
the far finger raised to the sky

and pointing out
different ways
in the moment's stopped air –
my black curly hair
almost like my master's.

England

History is now and England
– T. S. ELIOT, 'Little Gidding'

We all have lives that go on without us.
I've a cricket-me who didn't stop – like that
was that, when my bat had felt as heavy as England
and I took no wickets while the coach stood in my net
in the second and final trial for Warwickshire.
A bear and staff on my jumper, perhaps later . . .
But those butterflies. It thundered outside
on that second day. Life forks and stops
where another follows on. England's Moeen
Ali went to my school. His dad's from Dadyal.
Mine's up in the village over the bridge.
I don't know if he knows what I do now.
Dad I mean. We all have lives that go on
without us. Unwritten. I have history on grounds

I've not played on. Grace Road. The Oval. Eden
Gardens. We all have lives that go on without
us. It matters where the line breaks. I knew
I should pursue this future – that was almost
behind me, at the woods' edge, a realm between
weathers, where losses and times fold, at the crease –

clueless as to what it was. Or for who.

Nuclear Test

I knew it was the beginning of something.
My first match. History in the making –
the way history turns in the air like a coin –
creating a rupture. The first day Imran

captains his country. Dad and I in our seats –
on the morning of that double first Test –
behind the bowler's arm as he, the man
who'd be voted Prime Minister, the *Kaptaan*

with a cricket bat symbol on the ballot
turns at the border he marked with his boot
to deliver the first action I'd see, in godlike
moves I would go on to copy – jumping high

as I am doing in a photograph, two years on
barefoot in Kashmir, holding a stone wrapped
in cloth . . . As history heads back, face up, I ask
Who is he, Dad? His man turns. Runs in. Gaining

pace, history is bound. Then is in the air again.

Keepers

And then he was behind me like a butterfly
acting the keeper, saying I was out of my crease
and flapping two arms to stump me.
Bails invisibly airborne. Goners.

This is the story. One blue-skied morning of a Test
I arrived with my dad early at Edgbaston
feeling like the first people there, save the souls
on the gates. I was hoping to get autographs.
Dad saw a man in a finely pressed suit and said, loudly
in his loud accent – an accent with a hinterland, I suppose
just like that of the man he was gesturing to, as he passed –
Son, it's the *great* Brian Johnston.

I didn't know that he was Johnners –
voice of *Test Match Special* and that Sunday show
Down Your Way, which Mum kept on – who added *ers*
at ends, to send a word his way, as if all should fluidly go on
shortened or not, like showers. So, out clean-bowled
was out – cleaners! – and Blowers weren't ghostly flicks
of wind on still days, nor dandelion clocks, but his co-traveller
on the airwaves – the now late Henry Blofeld.

O, there's nothing so *great* about me, boomed Johnners.
I half knew his voice and didn't speak. This old dapper gent
who walked like he'd an appointment to keep, stopped
to sign my blank pad, taking a slow shine to me and my dad.
He wants to play for England one day, pronounced Dad.
I didn't nod. Still too shy to speak.

Johnners asked what my stance was. I placed my feet
and stood with an invisible bat. *Very* good! I felt like England
was talking to me. My eyes on England's two-tone brogue
shoes. That well-polished voice: *Show* me your *best* shot.
I still didn't speak, but swung like a small breeze
my long-stepped cover drive, and – not alive
to his wheeze – the ball had turned
past my bat and I apparently

was out of my crease.

Oval Hours

1

Empty cathedral –
Gasholder No. 1 – near
a full-housed Oval.

2

Time's haunting lattice –
history's (Grade II) cylinder –
its future listed.

3

The pigeon steps out,
one foot in the outfield, one
in radio chat.

4

Some space satellite
sends late night talk down under
on the spinner's *flight.*

5

He holds up the ball,
tilts the seasoned hemispheres.
Umpire, it wobbles.

6

Sixty seconds . . . six-
ball overs . . . Sonnet 60 . . .
curved time lord . . . *his scythe.*

7

Shakespeare caught The Globe;
his father was a seamer –
leather in the glove.

8

He scythes it over
mid on – *agricultural
shot* – to cow corner.

9

An attacking field –
catchers like stars round the pole –
that deep space they yield.

10

See the nightwatchman
spin his bat – sun on the blade –
summer, then autumn.

11

When bad light stops play
I think: since when is light *bad*?
What would Milton say?

12

Time's highest scorer –
invisible, ghostly, slow
clocker up . . . *Extras*.

Over

it's nothing really
just the way it is
or was said on the heels of me
getting into my stride

that oval long held   O
then a lifted skyward   *ver* –
after the last short
drop of the stone in hand

to the white coat pocket
– I still hear   O   *ver*   O   *ver*
when no one's there
to say it

far from that pocketed day
lost to the weather
on a loud grey beach
taking a blind sole

step away from the creased
sea when my boot heel
knocks back a shell
or a whitened

pebble that might just
as well be a wisp or the lonely
thought that I haven't connected
to anything

EXTRAS

For all your beginnings refuse to have an end
– JOHN GOWER, *Vox Clamantis*

Like as the waves make towards the pebbl'd shore,
So do our minutes hasten to their end
– WILLIAM SHAKESPEARE, 'Sonnet 60'

Fielder

If I had to put my finger on where this started,
I'd trace a circle round the one moment I came to, or the one
that placed me, a fielder, just past the field, over the rope,
having chased a lost cause, leathered for six . . .
when, bumbling about, obscured in the bushes,
I completely stopped looking for the ball –
perhaps irresponsibly – slowed by bracken, caught by light
that slipped the dark cordon of rhododendron hands,
a world hidden from the batsmen, the umpires and my team,
like the thing itself: that small, seamed planet, shined
on one half, having reached its stop, out of the sphere of sight.
And when I reflect, here, from this undiscovered city,
well north of those boyish ambitions – for the county,
maybe later the country – I know something of that minute
holds something of me, there, beyond the boundary,
in that edgeland of central England. A shady fingernail
of forest. The pitch it points at, or past, a stopped clock.
Still, in the middle, the keeper's gloves
clap at the evening. Still, a train clicks
on far-off tracks. And the stars are still to surface.
The whole field, meanwhile, waiting for me,
some astronaut, or lost explorer, to emerge with a wave
that brings the ball   like time itself   to hand. A world restored.
But what I'd come to find in that late hour
was out of mind, and, the thing is, I didn't care
and this is what's throwing me now.

Six

Forget that old joke about   timing, which I won't rudely
repeat. I learnt that timing had a world to do with weight
transference between the feet, planting my front pole
down, and as the ball is middled, the burden on the back
foot amasses through the axis of tensed, stick-thin arms
to the sweet spot in the rootless willow. A kind of sacrifice

from one side to the other. The ball now hit, and staying
hit – airborne, insanely towards a sky the locked-in
Scottish grandmother I'd never meet might have called
the lift. Over the fence, from that first garden
to another address, all that wound-up string beneath
the skin. Gone. *Mum's gone*, says Roseta, the girl at 60,

next to our 58, one morning while fetching the washing
from a line spiralling a shared stake. *Gone where?*
asks mine. *Where's your mother?*   *She's dead? Dear God.*
O, *Love*, Mum says above the crossed lines. At her tears
I'm still cottoning on. Roseta, Zeta, who posted
my first Valentine, signed with a question mark I'd not

get. Whose mum was *the only one* who could get me
to sleep. To the country of that eternal beginningness.
She'd come round in the small hours, Mum would say,
*hearing your cries, Dad working nights, and she'd go
like this, jigging you in her arms, and you'd be off, gone.*
She'd come from Barbados, her husband from Jamaica,

a one-time boxer; *different islands, different tempers,*
she'd tell Mum. Fighting leaked in and past walls.
Silences too. Belted up. Once, innocent, naked,
I placed my penis through that fence, peed – till he waved
a pitchfork; fathers fist-fought. Once, Zeta's dad shook
a crowbar. Mine raised Mum's school hockey stick.

Dad's middle finger smashed. Feeling gone. Forever.
He made me press a needle to test the dead, knuckled
centre. The nerves.   Gone. The word's weight returns
me to that fenced world, at this turning point – when
I hit the ball – up to a sun that bounces off the glass
of next door's greenhouse. A perfect still point, until

my heavenly high is shattered. And the sky falls in.

Made In . . .

To get me into the mood to write this, I'm listening to 'Mr Blue Sky' by Electric Light Orchestra. On repeat. 'Sun is shining in the sky / There ain't a cloud in sight.'

I must associate that song with Moseley in Birmingham, perhaps because summers were so bright there. Or maybe it's that Bev Bevan of ELO went to the same school as me. As did the comedian Jasper Carrott, the England cricketer Moeen Ali and the former Guantánamo detainee Moazzam Begg. 'Running down the avenue / See how the sun shines brightly in the city / On the streets where once was pity.'

I lived on College Road, very near Moseley school, in the same semi-detached house from birth to nineteen. Down the road was a small roundabout I was once stranded on as a child – a long story – and branching to the left was urban Sparkhill, which led to the city centre. The BBC comedy *Citizen Khan* proudly begins: 'Welcome to Sparkhill, Birmingham, the capital of British Pakistan.'

Up College Road and along the leafier Wake Green Road is the wooded Moseley bog, the other side of which is where J. R. R. Tolkien grew up. I was more interested in cricket than books – I had trials for Warwickshire before I gave up completely – and wouldn't have known about Tolkien's *The Lord of the Rings*, and that the woods up the road were his inspiration for the enchanted primordial Old Forest.

Along Wake Green Road in the other direction was eventually Edgbaston cricket ground, which was another kind of holy place for me, a green bucket of mixed memories. I'd go every summer to half watch matches as a young boy, often on my own, with a

Walkman and a cassette – usually the Beatles' *Magical Mystery Tour* – playing on my headphones.

I once saw Muhammad Ali there, who was visiting the nearby Central Mosque, and got his autograph, with my name on it and everything. My father was never prouder of me than when I came home with this, nor as disappointed as when I lost the shiny green Parka I used to carry the signature in, zipped into an arm pocket.

The memories that seem to hold me most are in green pockets, in gardens, parks, bits of woodland. Perhaps it's time's green pockets, as much as Moseley's. The first poem in my book *Us* begins with me as a boy, looking for a cricket ball beyond the boundary, in brambles – in 'a shady fingernail of forest' – having a moment where I can almost sense myself in the future looking back, looking for something. Which is how I feel, writing this now, with the same song still on repeat. 'Never mind, I'll remember you this way / Mr Blue Sky . . .'

My book ends with a blue sky above a tree I used to climb in my back garden in Moseley. I have a mad theory that the old forest of Arden has left an imprint somehow, zipped into the air, small pockets that fold worlds in. There was a hazy, wooded feel to the worlds I lived in, whether concreted over or not. I like how poetry can hold this mossy sense of folded-in worlds.

Folded within the leaves of *Us* are echoes from other books, including a snippet of Sendak's *Where the Wild Things Are*. It left an early imprint, with its forest that grew . . . and grew . . . and grew . . . 'and the walls became the world all around'. Where I grew up, on the Sparkhill edge of Moseley, did feel like the world all around.

And it still feels magical to me, even from this distance.

Zaffar Kunial was born in Birmingham and lives in Hebden Bridge. His debut collection, *Us* (2018), was shortlisted for a number of prizes, including the Costa Book Award for Poetry and the T. S. Eliot Prize. Since his first public reading, of 'Hill Speak' at the 2011 National Poetry Competition awards, Kunial has spoken at various literature festivals and in programmes for BBC Radio. In 2019, he was poet in residence at the Oval as part of the Places of Poetry project.

'barefoot in Kashmir, holding a stone wrapped / in cloth'